A Diff
to Wellness

Fun, Simple Ways to Create
a Happier, Healthier You

Renee Randazzese

2015

A Different Way to Wellness:
Fun, Simple Ways to Create a Happier, Healthier You
Copyright © 2015 by Renee Randazzese

To contact the author, visit:
www.ADifferentWaytoWellness.com

ISBN-13: 978-1508870159
ISBN-10: 1508870152

Printed in the United States of America

Printed by CreateSpace, An Amazon.com Company

Cover Design: Michelle Rau/Renee Randazzese
Artwork: Michelle Rau
Interior Design: Renee Randazzese

Dedications

This book is dedicated to my mom, Celia.

My best friend in life who understands me the most and always makes me laugh. Whom I love with all my heart and would be lost without....

To my Monster who makes me smile every day.

In Memory Of....

In memory of my dear friend Arlene Burns. We laughed, we sang and we danced. Every hour spent with you was a happy hour. I miss you Lady more than you know, but I can feel your light shining down upon me from above. Your passing reminds me to live each day as if it was my last. I know we will meet up again in the future, just remember to save me a seat at the bar.

Acknowledgements

I would like to thank Joshua Rosenthal and the Institute for Integrative Nutrition®. You have impacted my life beyond measure. Since joining the school, I have found a sense of purpose that had previously not existed. My life will be forever changed and I hope upon writing this book others' lives will be changed as well.

A special thanks to Dr. Ronald Sinagra and Dr. David Weinstein at Sunrise Wellness Center. Without your expertise, guidance, love and support, I would not have been able to attain the level of health and wellness that I have today.

Table of Contents

Copyright & Disclaimer

Dedications

In Memory Of

Acknowledgements

Introduction

Introduction

My goal in writing this book is simply to remind you of the things that came naturally to you as a child. An innate way of being that has been buried away deep down inside; a way which can be reignited. We didn't think about health as a child, we lived and breathed it. As children, we were joyful not mindful. As adults, we need to be mindful about being joyful. Within joy I believe is health. Consider this a mini "play" book that reminds you that a joyful approach to life is a healthy life. I use the four essential elements of life: Air, Water, Fire and Earth as a guideline. Are you ready to be transformed?

CHAPTER 1
Air

SOME BASIC FACTS....

"I believe that a simple and unassuming manner of life is best for everyone, best both for the body and the mind." - Albert Einstein

Air. Inhale, hold for a second, and now exhale. Now didn't that feel good? Just because we don't have to think about breathing doesn't mean we shouldn't be thinking about it. Taking in a good breath of air feeds our blood and nourishes our brain. So, wouldn't you want to get the most of each breath? Breathing is part of our autonomic nervous system (ANS).

Breathing occurs outside our conscious mind. The neat thing about breathing is, even though it occurs whether we think about it or not, we can consciously influence it. We can concentrate on deep breathing, which oxygenates our blood and calms our mind, or we can do aerobic exercise, which feeds our blood and gives us a burst of energy. We should practice both as air is the number one essential element for life. In the pages ahead, I will suggest some fun ways to get the most out of the air that surrounds you. Simple, joyful ways like laughing, singing and dancing as well as a wonderful breathing exercise. Enjoy.

SING

"I believe that singing is the key to long life, a good figure, a stable temperament, increased intelligence, new friends, super self-confidence, heightened sexual attractiveness, and a better sense of humor." - Brian Eno

Let's face it, singing is just plain fun. You don't need to be able to carry a tune and you can be completely tone deaf, you just need to sing. Sing in the morning

while you get ready for work; trust me you will have more energy and be in a better mood all day. Sing in the shower, the warm moist air will open up your sinuses. Sing in the car, so what if you look silly doing it. There are so many health benefits to singing. Singing exercises your lungs and brings more oxygen into the blood which improves circulation. It releases endorphins and elevates your mood. A familiar song can bring back long forgotten memories. It can make you think of an old friend you lost touch with; if that happens then act upon it and pick up the phone, or send a text or email. Singing can relieve tension, increase alertness and help relieve depression.

Singing is social. Grab a friend and go to a concert. Find a place that has a karaoke night. I cannot sing for my life, but something happens when you get on stage with your friends and you start belting out "*Paradise by the Dashboard Light*." You have to do karaoke at least once if your life.

If you are embarrassed, then go to a different town so there won't be a chance of anyone knowing you. Better yet, do it when you are on vacation. When my best friend got married in Vegas they had karaoke in the hotel bar. What better place to do it then in Vegas. If karaoke isn't your thing, then sing in church or your place or worship. It can be as simple as humming a tune or just whistling as you work.

On a side note, have you ever noticed that you can remember all the words to all the songs you have heard throughout your lifetime? Songs you haven't heard since you were young and when they come on the radio you remember all the words. You remember the words to new songs that are out now, but you don't remember where you left your car keys. Why is that? There is different scientific reasoning that attempts to answer that question; is it the lyrics or the melody? In my opinion we remember the words we sing because singing makes us feel good. It is just that simple and we should do what makes us feel good.

I remember when I was in the fourth grade I was in a play. I had to sing the 6 multiplication table. To this day I can still remember the words and the melody to that song. We remember songs in commercials and theme songs to TV sitcoms. What is your theme song? I challenge you to create a brief jingle about how you want to live each day or pick a lyric to a song that evokes feelings of happiness and joy and make it your mantra. When you are joyful you radiate good health; so sing to your health. Express yourself in song.

DANCE

"What if "the hokey pokey" is REALLY what it's all about?" – Curtis Spencer

Just dance. You can start off simply by tapping your foot or shaking your shoulders and before you know it you start moving to the beat. Dance is so great for your body. If you don't like to exercise then at least dance. You can do something formal like Zumba® or joining a Hip Hop class or you can dance in the privacy of your own home. Dance is so joyful and is great aerobic exercise.

Once again, it is one of those simple ways that you can incorporate into your everyday life that has a big impact on your health. When your children are dancing along to their favorite television show stop what you are doing and join them. You can even play your favorite music and have them join you. Turn the TV off and turn the music on when preparing dinner. Trust me, your food will taste better when it is infused with joy. Your energy will radiate through it.

Making dinner with your significant other with some great R&B music playing in the background can be so sexy. Take a minute or two in each other's arms while the sauce is simmering or the meat is resting.

When you get home from work don't turn on the news, turn up the tunes. Television sucks the life right out of you; you turn it on and life passes you by. When you turn on the music something magical happens and you become transformed. Your pulse speeds up, your hips start moving and you raise your arms overhead and begin swaying to the beat. Things get done. You are bouncing around and you decide you have the energy for that load of laundry or time to clean out that closet.

Dance has so many health benefits. It speeds up your metabolism and can help you lose weight or maintain a healthy weight. It tones your muscles in a gentle way, which is great for the elderly. It elevates your mood and can relieve depression. It lowers blood pressure, increases your stamina and helps strengthen your bones. Dance is a great way to reduce stress.

As with any exercise regimen, check with your doctor that you are well enough to partake in it. Once you have the green light, then two step or dosey doe to a happier, healthier you.

LAUGH

"Laugh my friend, for laughter ignites a fire within the pit of your belly and awakens your being." — Stella & Blake

Laughter increases the blood flow which is good for your heart and your brain. *"A good belly laugh leads to the release of endorphins from the brain," says Michael Miller, M.D., Director of the Center for Preventive Cardiology at the University of Maryland Medical Center in Baltimore.* Endorphins elevate your mood; what can be healthier than that?

I know when I am laughing I just feel better! When I go to work, I try to make my staff laugh every day. I take some time to connect with them, and putting them in a good mood benefits us all. I truly believe that it improves job performance and that if you can connect through laughter it forms a bond.

Have you ever gone to a comedy club with a group of friends? What a fun night out. Being part of an audience that is laughing in unison for an hour or two is therapeutic. You leave the club more alert than when you walked in. You feel happy and alive. You should want to feel like that every day. Make plans to go to the movies or rent a comedy at home and invite friends and family over to watch it with you. Laughter is contagious, so the more the merrier.

With the internet it is so easy to get a joke sent to your inbox. You can have one emailed to you every morning. I suggest starting your day with a funny joke or antidote and sharing it with as many people as possible. Tell your co-workers (make sure it's appropriate), pass it along to your friends and tell your mom and dad the next time you speak on the phone.

"The old saying that 'laughter is the best medicine,' definitely appears to be true when it comes to protecting your heart," says Michael Miller, M.D. and he suggests that *"thirty minutes of exercise three times a week, and 15 minutes of laughter on a daily basis is probably good for the vascular system."* Now that puts a smile on my face.

MY THOUGHTS ON MEDITATION

I believe that meditation can be transformative, but you have to find what works for you. I have tried traditional meditation and it doesn't work for me. My cousin and I started a 3 week challenge together and she enjoyed and benefited from it immensely, but I just couldn't quiet my mind. I lasted about one week, and then I gave up. When it comes to meditation and breathing I rather enjoy being more interactive. I know some will say it defeats the purpose but for those of you who are more like me, these are my personal suggestions.

Bodhi Meditation. My acupuncturist is also a healer and teaches Bodhi Meditation. I really enjoy it because it is more visual and you engage your body as well as your mind. Since I have a difficult time quieting my mind, focused, guided meditation and mental imagery works best for me.

Another way I enjoy breath work and the benefit of meditation is the practice of *Qigong.* Qigong is defined as "*an ancient Chinese healing art, involving meditation, controlled breathing, and movement exercises.*" You practice bringing energy towards and around you. It is quite fluid and mentally calming; but I must say, you can really work up a sweat.

The breathing technique that I benefit from is one recommended by *Dr. Andrew Weil* and is called the *"4-7-8 Breathing Exercise"*. The following excerpt was taken directly from his website.

"Practicing regular, mindful breathing can be calming and energizing and can even help with stress-related health problems ranging from panic attacks to digestive disorders." - Andrew Weil, M.D.

The 4-7-8 (or Relaxing Breath) Exercise

This exercise is utterly simple, takes almost no time, requires no equipment and can be done anywhere. Although you can do the exercise in any position, sit with your back straight while learning the exercise. Place the tip of your tongue against the ridge of tissue just behind your upper front teeth, and keep it there through the entire exercise. You will be exhaling through your mouth around your tongue; try pursing your lips slightly if this seems awkward.

- *Exhale completely through your mouth, making a whoosh sound.*

- *Close your mouth and inhale quietly through your nose to a mental count of **four**.*

- *Hold your breath for a count of **seven**.*

- *Exhale completely through your mouth, making a whoosh sound to a count of **eight**.*

- *This is one breath. Now inhale again and repeat the cycle three more times for a total of four breaths.*

Note that you always inhale quietly through your nose and exhale audibly through your mouth. The tip of your tongue stays in position the whole time. Exhalation takes twice as long as inhalation. The absolute time you spend on each phase is not important; the ratio of 4:7:8 is important. If you have trouble holding your breath, speed the exercise up but keep to the ratio of 4:7:8 for the three phases.

With practice, you can slow it all down and get used to inhaling and exhaling more and more deeply.

This exercise is a natural tranquilizer for the nervous system. Unlike tranquilizing drugs, which are often effective when you first take them but then lose their power over time, this exercise is subtle when you first try it but gains in power with repetition and practice. Do it at least twice a day. You cannot do it too frequently. Do not do more than four breaths at one time for the first month of practice. Later, if you wish, you can extend it to eight breaths. If you feel a little lightheaded when you first breathe this way, do not be concerned; it will pass.

Once you develop this technique by practicing it every day, it will be a very useful tool that you will always have with you. Use it whenever anything upsetting happens - before you react. Use it whenever you are aware of internal tension. Use it to help you fall asleep. This exercise cannot be recommended too highly. Everyone can benefit from it.

Dr. Weil's technique as explained above in his words is a wonderful way to still your mind and helps to release stress. Try incorporating it into your daily wellness program and experience the benefits.

SUMMATION

I stated in the beginning of this chapter, air is the number one essential element to life. There are ways to improve the quality of our breathing through mediation and exercises like Qigong. There are also simple steps to use our lungs in a fun and useful way such as singing, dancing and laughing that provide undeniable benefits to our health and well-being. They also form a connection between friends and loved ones and can be used as a daily dose of added joy to our lives.

My simple recommendations should be used as enhancements to improve your health and are not suggested to replace the benefits of traditional aerobic exercises, but should be used in conjunction with them.

CHAPTER 2
WATER

SOME BASIC FACTS….

Our bodies are made up of about 60% percent water and our brains are approximately 70% water. It is recommended that we drink 8-10 glasses of water a day because we need to replace what is lost through perspiration and elimination.

Water helps regulate our body temperature and keeps us hydrated, which is why it is so important to drink it while you exercise or on a hot, sunny day. Water keeps our joints lubricated and our brains functioning properly. Water is needed in the elimination process to help rid the body of waste and toxins. When burning fat, it is passed through the urine as Ketones. Water can also curb your appetite.

Water quenches our thirst; it is free of dyes and is readily available. We all have heard of the benefits of drinking water and that it is essential for proper bodily functions. In this chapter I will discuss the feel good factor of water. So sit back, and take a sip.

DRINK TO YOUR HEART'S CONTENT

To me there is nothing more refreshing or soothing than water. Water, tea and juicing are the only things I drink on a daily basis. I love water and drinking 8-10 glasses a day of that cool, crystal clear beverage is a no brainer for me. But for others, I know it can be a chore. Here are some ways to punch it up so you can drink it down.

Citrus Squeeze

So easy, yet very healthy for you. Lemons, limes, grapefruit and oranges contain vitamin C which helps support your immune system. It can help soothe a sore throat and when you drink warm water with lemon in the morning, it can aid in digestion. I like to mix it up. If I have oranges in the house, I will add a slice to my water. When I am in a restaurant, I ask for lemon water or sometimes water with lime. It is free, healthy for you and very tasty.

Simple Sangria

Slice up some apple and pineapple, cut up strawberries, pop in some blueberries or raspberries and add to a large pitcher of ice water. It makes for such a nice beverage in the summer to share with family and friends and even makes a beautiful centerpiece on the table.

Go Green

I like to pick mint and basil from my garden and tear the leaves up and add to my water. You can even add slices of cucumber for a cool, refreshing drink. Think mojito without the alcohol.

Specialty Blends

I really enjoy herbal teas. One of my favorites is *Yogi®* *"Green Tea Super Antioxidant."* When you begin to transition away from soda, I suggest trying herbal tea. It provides the sweet factor without the sugar. There are so many flavors and different blends. Look for organic ingredients with no added sugar or artificial flavors. I prefer using Stevia when I want a little extra sweetness. Also, different tea leaves have different caffeine content. I recommend researching the various types of tea.

Freeze It

I like to freeze my flavored tea into ice cubes to add to a glass of water in the summertime. I also make ice pops out of them like my mother did when I was a kid. Remember those molds? They still sell them today.

However you like it, hot or cold, plain or jazzed up, please drink more water. A hydrated body is a healthy body; it is as simple as that.

SELF CARE

Water plays such an important part of self-care. To me, there is more to a shower then just getting clean. It should be a spa experience just like when you take time out for a bath. Invest in some natural hair and body products that are free of chemicals and dyes. Look for organic ingredients and take the time to read the label. They may cost a little bit more, but not so much more and you will see that you don't need to use as much. Stretch in the shower while your muscles are relaxed from the heat and moisture. Sing, as it is joyful and you will end up stepping out of the shower with more pep and energy.

Another way to take care of you is with a *Hot Towel Scrub*. Below was obtained from the *Institute for Integrative Nutrition®*.

Hot Towel Scrub

Body scrubbing can be done before or after your bath or shower, or anytime during the day. All you need is a sink with hot water and a medium-sized cotton washcloth. For the maximum effect, scrub your body twice a day: once in the morning and once again in the evening. Scrub for two minutes to 20 minutes, depending on the amount of time you have. The process of the hot towel scrub has a deeper physical, mental, and emotional effect when done at the sink as opposed to in the shower.

Hot Towel Scrub Directions

- *Turn on the hot water and fill the sink.*

- *Hold the towel at both ends and place in the hot water.*

- *Wring out the towel.*

- *While the towel is still hot and steamy, begin to scrub the skin gently.*

- *Do one section of the body at a time: for example, begin with the hands and fingers and work your way up the arms, to the shoulders, neck and face, then down to the chest, upper back, abdomen, lower back, buttocks, legs, feet, and toes.*

- *Scrub until the skin becomes slightly pink or until each part becomes warm.*

• *Reheat the towel often by dipping it in the sink of hot water after scrubbing each section, or as soon as the towel starts to cool.*

Benefits

• *Reduces muscle tension.*

• *Reenergizes in the morning and deeply relaxes at night.*

• *Opens the pores to release stored toxins.*

• *Softens deposits of hard fat below the skin and prepares them for discharge.*

• *Allows excess fat, mucus, cellulite, and toxins to actively discharge to the surface rather than to accumulate around deeper vital organs.*

• *Relieves stress through meditative action of rubbing the skin.*

• *Calms the mind.*

• *Promotes circulation.*

• *Activates the lymphatic system, especially when scrubbing underarms and groin.*

• *Easy massage and deep self-care.*

• Can be a sacred moment in your day, especially if done with candlelight and a drop or two of essential oil, such as lavender.

• Creates a profound and loving relationship with the body, especially parts not often shown care, and especially for a person with body image problems.

• Spreads energy through the chakras.

© Integrative Nutrition | Reprinted with permission

Take the time for self-care and make your bath and shower time spa time.

TAKE A DIP

I think water is just plain fun. Go to the beach. I don't go into the water very far; just below my knee is my safe zone, but I love the ocean. The sheer vastness of it. The salt air and the sound of the waves crashing on the shore is simply invigorating. Even if you just take a drive down by the beach, it does something to you. If you don't live by the ocean, go to a lake or stream or go to a neighborhood duck pond. One of my favorite "me" dates that I enjoy is grabbing my camera and heading to the local duck pond. It's such a delightful day in the sun.

Go swimming. Swimming is such great exercise. It is easy on the joints, total body toning and can be aerobic or anaerobic depending on the intensity and duration of what you do. If you don't have a pool, find a local YMCA® in your area that has one. Most town parks have pools as well that you can join or just visit for the day.

Most of us know someone who has a pool, so invite yourself over. Truth be told, they probably aren't using it as much as they should and this would be a fun reminder. Invite them over to your house first and then ask them when their next pool party is and tell them you'll bring the salad. Relaxing in a pool on a float or a tube or hanging onto a noodle is so much fun. If you don't have a pool or have a friend that has one, then get yourself a sprinkler and invite your friends over for a sprinkler party. We used to love jumping through sprinklers when we were kids, so I say try it now. You may look silly doing it, but that only means that you are doing it right!

CHAPTER 3

FIRE

"Passion is energy. Feel the power that comes from focusing on what excites you." – Oprah Winfrey

When I speak of fire as an essential element, I am speaking about it metaphorically. I am speaking about the flame that burns inside you or once did. A passionate relationship, a fulfilling career, an active social life or a fun hobby or sport. Find what inspires you. It's time to turn up the heat and begin to sizzle!

BUST A MOVE

Why is it that so many of us no longer play? I envy those who love to exercise. I unfortunately, fall into the group that does not. So when it comes to exercise as I get older, I choose to do only what I enjoy because otherwise I won't stick with it. I think of exercise as play time.

In the summer I garden. I can garden all day long. I am so passionate about gardening. Gardening brings me happiness. I get to grow beautiful vegetables that I eat and share with family and friends. It is physical and dirty and pretty and tasty.

I like to go for walks. Walks by myself to reflect and rebalance. A walk with a friend to laugh and catch up. I am fortunate to live in an area that is close to parks and only a 10 minute drive to the beach. I also enjoy walking around my neighborhood. Find a place that is beautiful to take your walks and invite a friend. Go with a loved one and hold hands. Walks can be very romantic.

Ok, so what I am about to say next can be quite controversial; ready? I don't do yoga. Ok, I can hear the collective gasp. I know that yoga is great for you and there are many different kinds and that it is extremely beneficial. I highly recommend it and urge you to try it. I don't enjoy it, so I don't do it.

I suggest you search for something that you do enjoy that you don't consider work. If your doctor tells you that you need to exercise, then get a list of different types that he/she suggests and find what suits you best. Also, what you might have enjoyed in the past may not serve you at this point in time. I used to love to kick box, but not so much anymore. I try to find activities that fit where I am in my life right now.

I always carry a Nerf ® football in the trunk of my car. It is fun to toss around with friends. Maybe for you it is Frisbee® or flying a kite. Whatever you enjoyed as a child, chances are you will enjoy it as an adult and maybe even more so because you forgot how much fun it is.

FIND YOUR CALLING

What is your passion? What drives you or motivates you? Having a purpose or great relationships is much more important than counting calories when it comes to your health.

Think back to when you were a kid and it was summer. You could spend the entire day outside playing without a single thought of food. Your mom would call you in at lunchtime and you would have a quick bite, then out the door you went again. Being outdoors running around and playing with your friends is what nourished you.

What areas in your life need nourishment? If your social life is lacking, maybe join an organization that you are interested in. If it is spirituality, then seek out a traditional place of worship or maybe volunteerism will fill that need. Maybe it is education. There are great online courses or stop by your local library to see what they have to offer. Take the time to really figure out what is lacking in your life. If you focus on those areas and set intentions and follow through, your life will be more joyful. You won't be heading to the nearest fast food joint to fill that void anymore because it will no longer exist. No more dates with Ben and Jerry's® unless they are real people. When you find your calling (and you can have as many as you like), you will be living a meaningful life. Strive for balance. A life with purpose and meaning and passion is a healthy life.

SPREAD THE FLAMES

Once you find your passion, spread the flames. When I went back to school to become a health coach, it opened up an entirely new side of my personality that I didn't realize existed. I found a voice inside me that wants to help people. I found a passion within that I want to share with the world. That is the purpose of this book. I feel that it is the simple things in life that collectively, can have the greatest impact on health.

When you were just a toddler, you were taught your ABC's. First by sounding out the letter, then by word association and so on. Before long, you knew A is for apple and you could start forming sentences. I am not saying that if you have a major illness that flying a kite is going to cure you. What I am saying is that flying a kite is fun and uplifting and gets you off the couch and breathing fresh air and all of these things <u>are</u> healthy for you.

SUMMATION

If you are like most people reading this book, you are in a slump and have formed some bad, unhealthy habits over the years. By focusing on those things that excite you and sharing that excitement with others, you can create a whole new world for yourself. **I challenge you to start incorporating fun back into your life.** Share this "play" book with your family and take turns doing what each of you enjoys. Remember, when a family plays together, they stay together.

CHAPTER 4

EARTH

When I think of Earth as an element, I think of food. I like my food to be of the earth. Fruits and vegetables; nuts and seeds; whole grains and pure water. I won't be telling you that you should follow a certain diet or the latest trend like low carb or low fat. But what I do strongly believe in is eating local and buying organic. If you can grow it yourself than do so. If not, then shop your local farmer's market.

Join a CSA (community supported agriculture) or shop at a store that has an organic food section as the majority of them do these days.

The term organic can be confusing. The description below comes directly from the *AMS, USDA, National Organic Program, Consumer Brochure.*

"What is organic food? Organic food is produced by farmers who emphasize the use of renewable resources and the conservation of soil and water to enhance environmental quality for future generations. Organic meat, poultry, eggs, and dairy products come from animals that are given no antibiotics or growth hormones. Organic food is produced without using most conventional pesticides; fertilizers made with synthetic ingredients or sewage sludge; bioengineering; or ionizing radiation. Before a product can be labeled 'organic,' a Government-approved certifier inspects the farm where the food is grown to make sure the farmer is following all the rules necessary to meet USDA organic standards." "Companies that handle or

process organic food before it gets to your local supermarket or restaurant must be certified, too."

We as a society should not continue to support foods that are making us sick. The foods of today are not the foods that our grandparents ate. They may look the same but they are not the same. Food should be simple and be prepared from fresh ingredients and by your own hands. It is best to eat home cooked meals as often as possible, that way you know exactly what you are putting into your body. Meals need not be complicated; 5-6 ingredients tops. Experiment with fresh and dried herbs; try different leafy greens like mustard or Swiss chard. If you eat meat, make sure it is grass fed and pasture raised. Read your food labels. Here is an explanation of what the PLU codes on produce means.

Unlocking the Produce Code:

"One way to spot organic produce in the store is to check out each food's price look-up number or PLU. You'll find a PLU label on each piece of produce, attached as a sticker. The International Federation

for Produce Coding standardizes PLU codes for every grocery store in the country. Conventionally grown fruits and vegetables have 4-digit numbers and generally begin with a 3 or a 4. Organically grown fruits and vegetables have 5 digits and begin with a 9. Genetically modified fruits and vegetables also have 5 digits and begin with an 8. For example, the PLU for a conventionally grown banana is 4011; for an organic banana it's 94011; and for a genetically modified banana it's 84011."

Source: Adapted from www.plucodes.co

© Integrative Nutrition | Reprinted with permission

We need to eat to nourish our bodies to sustain our life. We control what we put into our bodies, but we tend to go on auto-pilot and make poor food choices. We need to take back control. In the next section, I will show you simple ways to incorporate healthy eating as a way of life.

IT'S A PARADIGM SHIFT

Paradigm:

"A set of assumptions, concepts, values, and practices that constitutes a way of viewing reality for the community that shares them, especially in an intellectual discipline."

We need to get out of this mindset that being healthy is hard and eating healthy is hard. We need to ignore the television touting the next flavored chip or 7 topping pizza. We need to learn to shop the outside perimeter of the supermarket only. Fruits and vegetables are generally on the right, meat and fish are in the back aisle and dairy is usually the outside left aisle. The only other aisle would be the bean and grain aisle. Check the internet to see if there is a local farmer's market in your area. Have you ever compared a store bought tomato to one that has been locally grown? There is no comparison; the locally grown tomato is bursting with flavor. If you stop buying the foods that are making you sick and start buying organic, real food, you would actually save money in the long run. No more wasting money on junk food that is unhealthy for you. You will save money on medicine and doctor's visits as well. Visit the *EWG.org* website and review the *"Dirty Dozen"* and the *"Clean Fifteen"* lists to educate yourself on what to always buy organic and what isn't necessary.

READ LABELS BUT DROP YOURS

It is important to read the ingredients on all your food labels. I buy an organic nut mix of almonds, cashews, walnuts and pistachios. When I look at the ingredients, it lists organic almonds, cashews, walnuts and pistachios. It is that simple. Food should be simple. If you don't know what it is, then don't buy it. If it contains sugar and high levels of sodium and dyes and partially hydrogenated oil and modified food starch, put the package down because it can only do you harm. Cakes, cookies, candy and bagels are made of sugar and starch which breaks down to sugar. An important thing to remember: it's **SUGAR** that makes you fat, **NOT FAT.** This is <u>key</u> folks. Fat is your primary source of fuel. Good, healthy fats are needed for energy, proper bodily functions and to keep you satiated. Healthy fats are olive oil, coconut oil, avocado, nuts and seeds. Your diet should include these fats along with fruits and vegetables plus healthy protein sources which include eggs, beans and lean, organic meat and fish.

When I wrote "read labels but drop yours" I meant the labels that we put on ourselves. Being sick and tired is no way to go through life. We should feel vibrant and radiate energy. When we eat real food grown in nature without pesticides and hormones, we can taste the difference and feel the difference. Locally grown fruits and vegetables contain a different energy than if they came from another state or country and forced to ripen in the back of a semi-trailer. The energy from local and organic food gets transferred into our cells. When we eat clean and green, we become one with the earth as nature intended us to be. Your body will thank you and reward you in health.

MY PERSONAL JOURNEY

In February 2014, I was overweight and so exhausted I could hardly move. I was working at a stressful job, living on caffeine, and eating processed foods. I was just plain sick and tired. I decided to find out what was wrong with me. I went to see a nutritionist who sent me for blood work. When my results came in, she said to me point blank if you don't lose weight immediately and start eating healthy you will have a heart attack or a stroke. I had metabolic syndrome, elevated levels of inflammation in my blood and was pre-diabetic. I had to make drastic changes immediately and I did.

My journey to recapture my health began the following month. I knew that I needed guidance since this wasn't just about losing weight, but also learning what was right for my body. So many mixed messages out there on what was healthy for you and what was not. I knew I needed someone more knowledgeable than I to hold me accountable. I hired a health coach. She taught me how to eat real food, and showed me how to recognize what foods worked for my body and what didn't. I saw immediate results eating real, delicious food and not depriving myself. I became so in awe of what my body can do. I lowered my LDL cholesterol, cut my triglycerides in half, and reversed my metabolic syndrome in just 4 short months. I was also taking supplements like fish oil and vitamin D which I was deficient in. (I recommend seeing your doctor or nutritionist to get a full blood work panel). At this point I knew I wanted to learn more about nutrition and help others like myself, so I went back to school and trained at Integrative Nutrition®.

Shortly after enrolling in school, I researched further into my health. I began suffering from debilitating Raynaud's attacks on a daily basis; I knew my journey wasn't over. With all that I have learned from school, that health and healing begins in the gut, I sought to find a doctor that could help me. I was fortunate enough to find two.

Dr. Ronald C. Sinagra and Dr. David B. Weinstein, pinpointed what was causing the inflammation in my body, and treated me metabolically. I ate REAL food and took quality nutritional supplements. NO MEDICATIONS like the traditional doctors wanted me to take. They treated me as a whole, and not just my symptoms. The results have been astounding and I am forever grateful.

I have been on an exciting and wonderful journey of transformation. In one year's time I have lost over 40 pounds, reversed my metabolic syndrome, I am no longer pre-diabetic, I have healed my gut, and reduced my inflammation. I learned the power of one's own body and the ability to heal. I became an Integrative Nutrition Health Coach and a published author. Incorporating all the different ways to wellness listed in this book led me to a journey of transformation, and I hope this can be the catalyst for you to begin yours.

CHAPTER 5
APPRECIATION

KEEP IT SIMPLE

Appreciation:

1. A feeling of being grateful for something; full awareness or understanding of something.

2. Recognition of the quality, value, significance or magnitude of people and things.

I like being appreciative versus being grateful. When I appreciate people, places and things, I feel fully engaged and present. When I say I am grateful for something, for some reason it makes me feel small. I want you to be the biggest, brightest self you can be.

When it comes to appreciation, there are simple ways to be mindful of it. You can create an inspiration box. You can cut out interesting articles or pictures. You can place a special birthday card you received in it. You can dry out a rose from a loved one and place it in your box. You can write down goals that you have achieved or photos from a family trip. You place whatever you want in that box. Pick a day, say New Year's Day to open the box and appreciate all that happened in your life throughout the year. If you have a spouse and kids, then every member of the family can have their own box and each can take turns sharing. From there you can paste what you want to keep into a scrapbook or photo album. Having something tangible that you can hold in your hands has a great impact on your soul.

Another way to be mindful of what you appreciate is to create a daily blog. When you were a kid, you couldn't wait to tell your mom and dad what happened at school that day. You couldn't wait to tell your friends about the adventures you had on your family vacation. Creating a blog is a way of sharing your appreciation with the world. If you are more of a private person, then old fashioned journaling may be the way to go. Writing is very cathartic and keeps you present. Pick yourself up a nice journal or you can even go to the dollar store and get yourself a notebook to write in. Find a time of the day that works for you when you can put your thoughts on paper. Don't make this a stressful event. Don't say I am going to write every night before going to bed or every morning right when I get up. Carry the book with you, and when you have a moment throughout the day, jot down that joke your boss told you or something that made you smile. Remember this is for you; it need not be perfect.

BED HEAD

When it comes to appreciation, you need to begin with a solid foundation. First, start with getting your bed in order. We need to address the end of your day before you begin your day. People should be getting 8-10 hours of sleep at night. Hitting the 10 hour mark is optimal, but no less than 7, even if you feel like you don't need it. Trust me, you do. Sleep is when your body repairs itself.

Get yourself soft, comfortable sheets. Then get yourself a blanket or comforter that you look forward to snuggling with. This is where appreciation comes into play, when you go to bed at night. I can't wait to dive under the covers. If you have a sleeping partner, make sure your bedding is big enough that neither of you are stealing the blanket. Also make sure it suits both of your requirements. If one is too hot and the other is too cold, neither of you will be getting the essential sleep that you need.

I would suggest having a large coverlet for display purposes and then peeling that back at night and each of you having your own bedding underneath. Start with a flat sheet that both of you are sharing; then say your partner likes it cool, their side of the bed would just have the flat sheet. You on the other hand like it hot, then get yourself a twin or baby blanket and have that draped over your side of the bed. This way both of you have the environment that suits your needs. Meanwhile, you two can and should snuggle underneath the flat sheet. Sleep should be restorative, not stressful, so figure out a set-up that caters to each of your needs. Remember, snuggling is just as important as sleep, so make time for that too.

The bedroom should be visually pleasing as well. Clean up the clutter! Find a proper home for what is lying on the floor or scattered on top of the dresser. The bedroom is your sanctuary, your place of peace. Choose colors that are pleasing to the eye and soothing to your brain. If you are single, make it your own retreat. If you share your room, you may have to compromise on the floral bedding or the lace curtains; remember both partners are sharing in this retreat and should feel equally at peace in it.

I recently had a vacation at a resort in Florida. I treated myself and splurged on a nice room. That bed was the most comfortable bed I have ever slept on. The room was so aesthetically pleasing that I knew I had to recreate it when I got home and I did.

I called the resort and asked what mattresses they used and I shopped around until I found one in my price range that delivered in comfort. It costs more for a better mattress, but this is a 10-15 year investment in your health. Shop at a store that offers interest free financing and get what your body needs. I also upgraded my pillow. A pillow is so individual; one size does not fit all. This does take time. I spent probably two months going to stores and trying out their beds and pillows until I finally got it right. Even if you go to one of the chain mattress stores, shop at their multiple locations, as some feature different models than others based on the demographics of what sells in that area.

With a little time and effort, I recreated the bed of my dreams and decorated my room in soothing warm browns and framed photography (some of my own) that evoked pleasant memories. Now when I go to bed at night, I can't wait to slip under the covers because I know I will have a great sleep. Remember, after a great sleep comes a great day so make this investment. Even if you can't afford the mattress just yet, start with your pillow or even a pillow top cover to put over your existing mattress. You deserve a great sleep and your body will thank you for it in improved health and well-being.

RISE AND SHINE

Keeping it simple when it comes to appreciation is the quickest and easiest way to bring joy and balance into your life. I start first thing in the morning, when I open my eyes. I wake up happy to be alive. I have a chance to hit the reset button. Just think when you turn the alarm button off, that is your opportunity to turn your life back on. **Your Life should be a TURN ON not a turn off!**

Before you start scrambling to get ready for work or get your kids off to school, take some time for yourself. Even if you only have a few minutes, make them your own. A few push-ups against the bedroom wall to get the blood flowing. Practice the breathing technique as described in chapter 2. Play your favorite music while taking a shower and don't forget to sing. The bathroom is a great place to steal some alone time. Practice hot towel scrubbing as a way to appreciate your body.

If you like journaling, the morning is a perfect opportunity to write. Even if you only have 10 minutes, take the time. Putting your thoughts on paper or in your iPad® gives you a sense of focus and clarity. Get moving. Grab your neighbor and go for a walk. A few laps around the block while the coffee is brewing will give you more energy than the coffee. Most people are lacking in Vitamin D, especially if you live in the northeast, where I come from. Your body needs it for proper health and well-being. Taking your walk outdoors is a great way to get some.

Get juicing. I love juicing and it is a quick and easy way to get your essential vitamins and minerals, as well as a healthy breakfast. I prefer using a NutriBullet®. They have wonderful pre-packaged super-foods that are available online that I add to the fresh fruits and vegetables that I use. Remember to mix it up and try experimenting with different combinations. You can also add powered protein and unsweetened almond milk and make yourself a smoothie.

Taking time for yourself in the morning is so important to your health. When you wake, take the time to appreciate yourself by practicing self-care, journaling, movement and proper nutrition. It doesn't need to be complicated; simply begin by turning on the radio and start singing along.

THE POWER OF THE REMOTE CONTROL

"I hope everyone that is reading this is having a really good day. And if you are not, just know that in every new minute that passes you have an opportunity to change that." – Gillian Anderson

Our thoughts control our feelings, it is that simple. We may praise or blame (usually blame) our moods or how we feel on things or events that are outside of ourselves. We need to remember that we control our emotions and how we react to people and situations is entirely up to us. **We have the power. We hold the remote and we can change the channel anytime we want.** We may initially react badly or get upset at something or someone, but we do not have to carry it with us throughout the entire day. Remember just change the channel.

Here is an example of how I recently changed the channel when it came to driving. I have to admit that I have used a choice word or two in the privacy of my own car to the driver who cut me off or who wouldn't allow me to merge into a lane. I have since adopted a newer approach to driving.

I think of the people in the cars that surround me as my family. I need to protect them and they need to protect me. We are in this together and by working together we will get to our destinations safely. By treating them as family, I find I am more kind, more forgiving, less reactive and definitely a much calmer driver. By making this simple shift in my mindset, I arrive at my destination in a pleasant mood and not ranting about some bozo who has just cut me off.

You have the power to make these little shifts and adjustments in your life. Just because you may have done something one way or reacted in one way for so long does not mean you can't change now. You have the power to transform and it is never too late.

THE PRACTICE OF BEING PRESENT

"Most people are prisoners, thinking only about the future or living in the past. They are not in the present, and the present is where everything begins."
– Carlos Santana

Do you remember when you were a child how the days seemed to last forever and time stood still? That's because we didn't wish our lives away. We lived in the present and stayed in the now. We lived by our senses and our priority was to enjoy life. When we were children we had to ask our parents' permission to do the activities we wanted to do to make us happy. Can we go to the park? Can I go in the pool? The silly thing is now that we are adults and we don't have to ask permission anymore, we forget to play. Just think, we can go to the park anytime we want.

Yes, we may have jobs and responsibilities that get in the way, but we can plan our play dates and we should. Mix it up, some by yourself, some with your partner, some with your family and some with your friends. Make a commitment and put it on the calendar. Be creative; if your husband likes to watch football on Sundays and you don't, don't get mad get playing. Pick up the phone and call your girlfriend that you haven't spoken to in months. Take in a movie with your mom or get a pedicure with your sister. This is the perfect time to experiment with that new recipe that you wanted to try out or to read a good book.

Play dates are so good for your soul. When you are happy, you feel fulfilled and you take better care of yourself. When you play, you are laughing and being active and you are using your senses. If you have children, you have a ready to go playmate; how great is that? Don't feel like it is a burden or a chore that you have to drive your child here and there to attend an event. Live through their eyes and share in their excitement.

Practice being present everyday of your life. It is when you learn to appreciate the little things that joy and happiness will manifest and become available to you. Be open to it and embrace it.

CHAPTER 6
SURRENDER

FORGIVE AND FORGET

"To forgive is to set a prisoner free and discover that the prisoner was you." — Lewis B. Smedes

When I speak of forgiveness in this book, I am focusing on forgiving oneself. I believe you should forgive others, but you have to forgive yourself if you want to be free. Free from doubt and self-criticism. Free from uncertainty and lack of confidence. Free from not obtaining your goals and becoming your true, authentic self. When I say you should forgive and forget, I mean once you forgive yourself then let it go. It is gone, forget about it, and move on! My approach when it comes to forgive and forget is this...

Think of today as your first chance to get it right, and your second chance to let it go.

Every day is a do over and don't you ever forget that! If you had a donut yesterday, so what because today is a do over. Today you have a brand new chance to get it right. Just think of how powerful that is. You can acknowledge that what you did yesterday was not in your best interest. Then forgive yourself and move on. You get to hit the reset button. Only you have the power over you. You may think it is food or poor health and you may feel like there is no hope. You may be so addicted to sugar or saturated fats and drive-through windows that you don't know how to break these self-destructive habits. Start with forgiveness to break the cycle.

Our poor food choices are usually a form of self-medication. What may have started off as a treat as a child, somehow becomes distorted as we grow up. When we get hurt we turn to food. If we miss out on a big promotion we turn to food. We need to get our support and love from people not food. **Food sustains our bodies, but people sustain our souls.**

Forgive your past in order to protect your future. You need to let go of toxic energy and emotion to allow yourself to be happy and healthy.

TIME FOR TRANSFORMATION

Can you recall when you were little how you were brimming with spirit and enthusiasm? You didn't have to think about it or have to work hard at it, it just came naturally. When you were a child every day was an exploration. You learned new words and went to new places and made new friends. You built things, you played in the mud and you twirled in circles until you fell down into a pile of giggles. You had not a care in the world and you didn't worry about tomorrow.

As adults we wish our lives away waiting for it to be 5pm on Friday so we can break for the weekend with the hope of having a little fun. It doesn't have to be that way if you carry out the suggestions outlined in this book. Your time is now. Take my hand and please join me on this journey to transformation.

When you wake up in the morning, perform your breathing exercise. Take a quick walk before hopping in the shower. Before hopping into the shower put on some music. If you can't take a walk, then do a little dance. Tell your children how beautiful they are each and every day. Don't forget to kiss your loved one goodbye. Hold the door open for a stranger. Let someone merge in front of you in traffic. Be generous and kind. When you step outside, take a deep breath of fresh air. Take a moment to appreciate the warm sun, blue sky or the magnificent storm clouds. Stretch. Stretch throughout the day as it is the easiest way to relieve tension. Stretch your arms far and wide; roll your shoulders front and back. It is a simple way to feel good. Eat real food and avoid chemicals. Stay hydrated! You water your plants and your lawn so remember to water your most important piece of property that you own and that is you!

Don't make a "TO DO" list make a "TODAY I WILL" list.

It should read something like this:

TODAY ✳ I WILL™

- ✳ Laugh
- ✳ Sing
- ✳ Dance
- ✳ Treat my body with respect
- ✳ Call an old friend, send mom flowers, make a "play" date, hug my loved ones, etc...
- ✳ Then you can fill it with work, school & errands

Joy Always Comes First!

Do you remember the game Hide and Seek? Well it is time to stop hiding from the happy, healthy, joyful life you deserve and it is time to start actively seeking it. You better start now because:

TAG YOU'RE IT!

REFERENCES

Anderson, Gillian. "Gillian Anderson Quote." BrainyQuote. Xplore, n.d. Web. 11 Mar. 2015.

"Appreciation." *Merriam-Webster*. Merriam-Webster, n.d. Web. 20 Feb. 2015.

"Bodhi Meditation: How to Practice." *Bodhi Meditation Society.org*. N.p., n.d. Web.

Einstein, Albert. "Albert Einstein Quote." BrainyQuote. Xplore, n.d. Web. 16 Feb. 2015.

Eno, Brian. "Brian Eno Quote." *BrainyQuote*. Xplore, n.d. Web. 9 Feb. 2015.

"EWG's Shopper's Guide to Pesticides in Produce™." EWG's 2015 Shopper's Guide to Pesticides in Produce™. N.p., n.d. Web. 28 Mar. 2015.

"Going Organic." *Agricultural Marketing Service*. N.p., 8 June 2010. Web. 16 Feb. 2015.

"Green Tea Super Antioxidant." *Green Tea Super Antioxidant* at Yogi. n.d. Web. 2 May 2015.

Meatloaf, and Ellen Foley, perfs. Paradise by the Dashboard Light. By Jim Steinman. Meatloaf. Rec. 1977. Todd Rundgren, 1976. Vinyl recording.

Miller, Michael, M.D. "Laughter Is the Best Medicine for Your Heart." *University of Maryland Medical Center*. N.p., n.d. Web. 10 Feb. 2015.

Miller, Michael, M.D. "On the Many Benefits of Laughter." *Laughter Online University*. N.p., n.d. Web. 10 Feb. 2015.

"Paradigm." The Free Dictionary. Farlex, n.d. Web. 21 Feb. 2015.

"Qigong." *Merriam-Webster*. Merriam-Webster, n.d. Web. 10 Mar. 2015.

Rosenthal, Joshua. "Hot Towel Scrub." Institute for Integrative Nutrition. N.p., n.d. Web. 11 Mar. 2015.

Rosenthal, Joshua. "Unlocking the Produce Code." *Integrative Nutrition: Feed Your Hunger for Health & Happiness*. 3rd ed. N.p.: Rosenthal, Joshua, 2014. 62. Print.

Santana, Carlos. "Carlos Santana Quote." BrainyQuote. Xplore, n.d. Web. 11 Mar. 2015.

Sinagra, Ronald C., D.C., and David B. Weinstein, D.C. *Http://sunrisechiropracticwellnesscenter.com/*. N.p., n.d. Web.

Smedes, Lewis B. "Lewis B. Smedes Quote." BrainyQuote. Xplore, n.d. Web. 11 Mar. 2015.

Spencer, Curtis. "Curtis Spencer Famous Quotes." *Curtis Spencer Famous Quotes*. N.p., n.d. Web. 9 Feb. 2015.

Stella & Blake. "Laughter Links & Quotes." *Thecenterofjoy*. N.p., n.d. Web. 10 Feb. 2015.

Weil, Andrew, M.D. "Spirit & Inspiration." *Breathing: Three Exercises*. N.p., n.d. Web. 09 Feb. 2015.

Winfrey, Oprah. "Oprah Winfrey Quote." *BrainyQuote*. Xplore, n.d. Web. 16 Feb. 2015.

Made in the USA
San Bernardino, CA
15 June 2015